It's About TIME!

5 Steps to True Time Management

**A practical how to guide
with all the tools you need**

JAMES R. BALL
JENNIFER A. KUCHTA

KEEP IT SIMPLE FOR SUCCESS®

It's About TIME!
5 Steps to True Time Management

ISBN: 1-887570-09-8

Published by The Goals Institute.
email:info@goalsinstitute.com

www.goalpower.com
www.goalsinstitute.com
www.kissbooks.com

Keep It Simple for Success®
is a registered trademark of The Goals Institute.

Please contact us for information about our seminars and
train-the-trainer materials on the contents of this book.

Printed in the United States of America
10 9 8 7 6 5 4 3 2 1

Dedication

Jim:

In memory of Ron and Betty Gawrych who made time for me early in my career when I needed their love, guidance, and encouragement the most. I miss them and will be forever grateful for their friendship and belief in me.

Jennifer:

For my very special friends Cheryl Mason, Barb Pomnitz, and Cindy Unangst with whom I have had some of the best times of my life and who always have time for me.

We also dedicate this book to all of the people who take time to love and help others.

Thanks and Appreciation

WE WANT to thank the following people:

Thanks to our friend Maggie Bedrosian for your creative ideas and true advice for the title and subtitle.

Thanks to our friend David Greenspan for your wisdom, guidance, and suggestions for improving the content and the way it is presented.

Thanks to our friend Ann Hunter, at AAH Graphics, for your editorial help in polishing our message.

Thanks to our friend Julie Young, at Young Design, for your ideas and graphics support on the cover.

Thanks to our clients and friends for the time you took to provide the valuable input we requested for the title of this book. Without your input, this book would not be *It's About TIME!*

Readers note: We based the examples and illustrations in this book upon facts and experiences that we observed or learned firsthand. To maintain the anonymity of individuals and companies we used pseudonyms and modified descriptions as required.

What Is In This Book for You?

CONGRATULATIONS! *It's About TIME! 5 Steps to True Time Management* contains valuable techniques and advice that will help you understand the importance of time and manage your time better so you are in control.

These techniques will help you **put more freedom, fun, and flexibility into your schedule**. You will be able to spend more time the way you want to spend it.

You also will learn how to stay more focused and work smarter so that you **achieve more in less time**.

The *5 Steps to True Time Management* provide a **simple roadmap to success**. We have been teaching these *5 Steps* for years and have seen the positive impact they have had on people's lives. Many individuals have told us that our unique seminar on these *5 Steps* is the best course they ever had. They often ask us, "Why didn't someone teach us this before?"

We know from experience that you will get results when you follow the *5 Steps*.

Best wishes for great success and happiness!

James R. Ball

Jennifer A. Kuchta

Contents

Contents

> *Time is the one thing that can never be retrieved. One may lose and regain a friend; one may lose and regain money; opportunity once spurned may come again; but the hours lost in idleness can never be brought back to be used in gainful purposes.*
>
> —C. R. Lawton

Just Take It

You are never going to find the time you are looking for, because it is already here and what you must do is take it.

Don't wake up tomorrow morning and say, "Here I am day, take me!" For the day surely will take you, if you let it.

Instead, wake up tomorrow morning and say, "Here I am day! This is what I am going to do."

Then seize the day with all your might and take it.

—Jim Ball

Time Management
and the 5 Steps

What I know for sure is that how you spend your time defines who you are. I try not to waste time—because I don't want to waste myself.

I control what I do with my time. We all do, even when it seems out of control.

Protect your time, it is your life.

—Oprah Winfrey
O, The Oprah Magazine

"Thou Art Mortal"

JULIUS CAESAR supposedly had a servant follow him around to remind him of his mortality.

This servant would periodically hold a laurel wreath above Caesar's head and say, "Thou art mortal."

This sounds strange; however, it shows us that Caesar grasped what many people never appreciate.

When our time runs out, we run out.

Caesar understood that it is easy to forget the importance of time. Time is life and life is time.

To put time into perspective think of the time in your life as the sand in an hourglass.

At birth, we each turned over our "hourglasses of life." Immediately, the minutes and hours available in our lives began dropping in a steady stream from the top chamber into the bottom chamber.

None of us knows how many hours we began with in the top chamber or how many we have left.

However, we all know this: Someday the few final grains in the top chamber will fall into the bottom chamber. We are mortal, too. Just like Caesar.

> *That is not sand dropping through the hourglass, that is you!*

—Jim Ball

Introduction to the 5 Steps

OUR APPROACH to managing time better and getting more done is the *5 Steps to True Time Management*. We often refer to these simply as the *5 Steps*. They are:

> Step 1: Make Choices and Set Goals
>
> Step 2: Know Where Your Time Goes
>
> Step 3: Plan Your Weeks
>
> Step 4: Make Each Day Count
>
> Step 5: Work Smarter

In our system, you only have to apply five steps and use three pieces of paper to manage your time better.

We also recommend that you use a calendar to keep track of appointments and a personal journal to record your progress. Nothing else is required. You do not need a planning system or electronic scheduler.

If you prefer to use software or a notebook calendar and planner, that is fine, but they are not required.

In the following chapters, we present each of the steps along with tips and suggestions for applying them.

Three forms: In three of the steps, we introduce a suggested form to apply the step. We refer to these three tools as *The Three Magic Pieces of Paper*. We have provided illustrations of each of these forms along with a recap of the instructions for completing them in the chapter entitled *The Three Magic Pieces of Paper*.

Time Management 101

THERE IS NO such thing as time management. We cannot slow time down, speed it up, or create it.

While we cannot manage time, **we can manage how we spend ourselves while time passes**.

To manage our time we must take control of our lives. Time management is self management.

Therefore, we refer to self management and time management in this book as one in the same.

Fundamental Principle

The fundamental principle of time management is that in order to "get time," you must take it.

No one is going to come up to you and say, "Here is an hour for you to do whatever you want to do."

What occurs in life is just the opposite. People say, "Do you have five minutes?" Before you know it, those five minutes become hours.

You must take control, or people will spend your life the way they want to spend it, not the way you choose.

To get time, take it: If you want an extra hour to do something that you want to do, then do not wait for someone to give you the hour. That will never happen.

Instead, just take the hour and do what you want to do. Do not wait for the hour to arrive. Take it now.

Make the Commitment

TO MANAGE your time you must make the commitment to do what is required.

Decide right now to take control. Say to yourself, *My time is my life. I am serious about taking control. I will make choices for how I spend myself.*

Make the commitment. Say to yourself, *I understand that in order for me to manage my time I must manage myself. I am committed to developing good skills and habits to manage my time and myself well.*

Pay Attention to the Minutes and Hours

Many people have a macro concept of time. They think of time as days, weeks, months, and years.

We live our lives, however, on a micro basis. We make choices and spend ourselves in minutes and hours.

If you manage your minutes and hours, your days, weeks, months, and years will take care of themselves. However, if you do not manage your minutes and hours, you have no chance of managing your days, weeks, months, and years.

Think about this. If you had just one extra hour a day for a year that is 365 hours. This is as much time as 45 eight-hour days. That is nine workweeks. Think what you could do with that extra time!

Dos and Don'ts

Do:

- Remember, Thou art mortal.
- Decide right now to take control of your time by managing yourself better.
- Get a notebook and set up a personal journal. You can use a spiral, loose leaf, perfect bound, or any kind of notebook you like.
- Enter the commitments that are presented in italics on page 6 in your journal. Include the date for each of your journal entries.
- Keep your journal on an ongoing basis. Jot down brief notations daily of how you spent your time and specific steps you intend to take to improve how you manage your time.

Don't:

- Get frustrated or give up if you cannot take control of your time immediately. Be persistent. Little by little, you will get in control and achieve the results you want.

Be avarice of time; do not give any moment without receiving its value; only allow hours to go from you with as much regret as you give to your gold; do not allow a single day to pass without increasing the treasure of your knowledge and virtue.

—Le Tourneux

Step 1:
Make Choices and Set Goals

Set Time Goals
with a 1-2-3 Approach

THE FIRST step to true time management is to set specific time management goals that you intend to take action to achieve. **This is the most important step by far**.

Unfortunately, many people who want to manage their time better either skip this step or do a poor job on it. They act before they think. They start changing things when they have only a vague idea of what they want.

It does no good to save time if you do not spend the time you save the way you want to spend it.

It also does no good to have time management goals that are not specific, because your brain cannot act on those goals. You will not be able to implement a goal like "I want to spend more time exercising" until you tell your brain what you mean by "more time."

In addition, it does no good to have time management goals unless you intend to act to achieve them.

We recommend a three-part approach for setting specific time management goals:

1. Stop and think about what you really want.
2. Set priorities and make decisions.
3. Turn your decisions into specific time management goals.

Stop and Think About
What You Really Want

A KEY TO making good choices about how you want to spend your time is taking time to identify your alternatives and think about them.

Time Want List: Set aside an hour or so of quiet time and prepare a list of Time Wants. List the things you want to spend more time on than you do currently.

Then think about the impact that spending additional time on these things would have.

A question to start with is, *What specifically do you want to do with your time that you are not doing now?*

Do you want to spend more time in some form of physical exercise? Imagine the impact this would have on your vitality and how long you will live.

Do you want to spend more time with your spouse, partner, children, parents, or friends? Imagine how this extra time could improve your relationships and enhance the contributions you can make to each other.

Do you want to spend more time reading and learning? Imagine how much more you could achieve over a lifetime with the additional knowledge you would gain.

Do you want to spend more time on important tasks at work? Imagine the impact this could have on your results, career advancement, and income.

Set Priorities and Make Decisions

ONE OF THE biggest problems people have in managing their time is prioritizing their alternatives so they can make good choices.

The next task, therefore, is to prioritize your time wants and decide which ones you are serious enough about to take action and make changes.

Select Your Top Three Priorities

Go over your Time Want list and select the top three time wants that you really want to achieve. These are the time wants you are serious enough about to act upon.

While you may have many time wants, we recommend that you first focus on no more than three. Stick with these until you are achieving the results that you want to be achieving. Then move on to more items.

Example: Anthony's Top Three Priorities

Anthony, a financial planning professional in one of our seminars, decided that his top three time wants were:

1. Spend more time with my family.
2. Spend more time at the gym.
3. Spend more time visiting with current clients and meeting prospective new clients.

Turn Your Decisions into Specific Goals

AFTER YOU HAVE decided your top three time wants, the next task is to turn your decisions into specific goals and strategies.

Quantify What You Want to Achieve

In order to set specific time management goals, you have to quantify your top three time wants.

Think through how much time you are spending on each activity now, and make a decision about how much time you want to be spending on that activity on an on-going basis. These are your time management goals. Record them in your journal.

You have a better chance of spending your time the way you want to spend it if you set clear and specific time management goals than if you do not. Anthony's examples below illustrate how to do this.

Anthony with His Son

When Anthony thought more about his goal of spending more time with his family, he decided that what he really wanted was to spend more time with his young son. He said this was his number one priority.

We asked Anthony how *much* more time he wanted to spend with his son. We also asked what he would do with that time.

Anthony had no ready answers.

After just a little discussion and thought, Anthony decided he had two goals. First, on non-travel week-nights his goal was to be home for at least an hour before his son went to bed. His second goal was to spend two Sunday mornings a month in learning-playing activities with his son. He called these his *Son*days.

Anthony wrote these two goals in his journal. Now his goals are clear, simple, and easy to remember and apply. The chances are good that Anthony will spend more time with his son with these clear goals in mind than he would have spent without them.

Anthony's Other Two Priorities

The examples below illustrate how Anthony quantified his other two top priorities.

Anthony's goal for time at the gym: "My goal is to get in a 60-minute workout at the gym from 6:00 a.m. to 7:00 a.m. each Monday, Wednesday, and Friday."

Anthony's goal for time with clients and prospects: "My goal is to spend at least two hours every day in face-to-face meetings with existing clients or new prospects."

Dos and Don'ts

Do:

- Stop and take time to think through your alternatives and time wants.

- Prioritize your time wants and select your top three to act upon.

- Quantify your top three time wants and turn them into specific goals.

Don't:

- Set vague or general goals for managing your time. Instead, set specific and clear goals that you actually can do.

Time is all we have.

—Ernest Hemingway

Step 2:
Know Where Your Time Goes

Where *Does* Time Go?

VERY FEW PEOPLE really know where their time goes.

We may think we know how we are spending our time, but how we *think* we spend our time is usually very different from what *actually happens*.

There have been many studies to determine how people actually spent their time in comparison to both how they planned to spend their time and how they think they spent it.

In case after case, individuals believed that they had spent their time the way they had planned to spend it. However, upon analysis, their actual time expenditures were quite different from what the individuals had thought they were.

Executive time study: Peter Drucker, the famous business sage, narrated a time management training video years ago. He demonstrated that people do not know how they are spending their time.

The video showed a time study where an executive estimated how he would spend his time for a week. Researchers then tracked his time in a log during that week.

At the end of the week, the researchers asked the executive how he thought he had done. The executive said he thought he had spent his time the way he had planned.

Much to the executive's surprise, his time log contained very different results. He had spent only a fraction of the time he had planned to spend and thought he had spent on an important business matter. Yet on unimportant matters he spent considerably more time than he had planned to spend or thought he had spent.

Salesperson time study: We conducted a study of how much time during a one-week period each of four salespersons spent in an actual *selling mode*. We defined a selling mode as time spent on the telephone or in person with an individual who could buy.

Our records showed that on average the four individuals had spent less than four hours each in a true selling mode for the entire week!

When we showed the salespersons our results, they were shocked. They had been fooling themselves and they did not know it.

We all fool ourselves: The executive and the four salespeople above are not the only ones who fool themselves. We all do. We all think we spend our time differently than we actually do.

Factual feedback: The key ingredient here is *factual* feedback. If you do not know where you are and where you are going, you cannot make good decisions.

Feedback on how you are spending your time is essential if you want to manage your time better.

Log Your Time

THE FEEDBACK tool we recommend to help you know where your time goes so you can manage it better is a **daily time log**.

We recommend that you prepare a daily time log for two or three days periodically, as needed, to maintain control over your time and be effective.

Most people resist when we recommend a time log. They say, "Is that necessary?" "Won't that take a lot of time itself?" "What will I learn from a time log that I do not already know?"

None of the excuses implied in questions like these is valid.

Preparing a time log takes very little time and it is easy and simple. We both have prepared many time logs for our own time, and we have hundreds of clients who use them as well. It only takes a few minutes throughout the day to maintain a time log.

New and Important Feedback

We do not know what we do not know about how we spend our time until we prepare a time log to reveal our realities.

Once when Jim prepared a time log he realized he was spending almost a third of his time on civic and charitable activities when he had important business and family matters that needed his attention. He had no idea he was spending that much time on those activities. His time log analysis helped him make good decisions and implement changes quickly.

Jennifer loves the time log technique and uses it often. Her time log provides continuous feedback to help her pace her work and stay on track during the day. She also keeps a time log when she finds herself time stressed or unfocused and wants to rebalance, refocus, and maximize her productivity.

College students: When we taught a class at George Mason University, we required students to prepare time logs for two full weeks. The students complained and offered all the excuses described earlier, and more.

However, after the first week numerous students told us about how they had made changes because of what they had learned. Many students told us that they could not believe how much time they had spent watching television, hanging out with friends, and partying. They also were surprised to learn how little time they actually were spending in class and studying.

"I don't have a life!" is how one student put it after she realized how much time she was wasting.

Many students said that they changed their television, partying, and studying habits substantially after completing their time logs.

Time logs provided the students with the *factual feedback* they needed to make good decisions.

How to Maintain a Time Log[*]

TO USE the time log technique, pick a typical week to record how you spend your time. The minimum period we recommend is two to three consecutive days.

By entering your time in a log, you will be aware of how you are spending your time. You will adjust your pace and actions and be more effective immediately.

Getting started: Either download our time log form or line off a pad of paper into the columns shown below.

Record your time during the day by adding a new entry each time you change activities. Here is an example of a partial time log for Maria.

Begin	End	Minutes	Activities/Tasks
8:00	8:15	15	Read the paper
8:15	8:25	10	Chat with Pat
8:25	8:45	20	Email

The more specific the information you record, the better. Maria could have expanded the second entry above to "Chatted with Pat about last night's concert." This would clarify that the discussion was social.

---

[*] Also, see the chapter, *The Three Magic Pieces of Paper*, where we provide an illustration of a Daily Time Log form, a recap of related preparation instructions, and information on how to download a free Daily Time Log form from The Goals Institute.

Maria also could have expanded the third entry to say "Email – took 10 minutes to reply to Sue's request for the Acme proposal." Details like this can help identify obstacles and opportunities to make changes.

Pacing: Notice that while the above time log contains only three entries, Maria can already see that she has spent nearly an hour of her 8-hour day and accomplished very little. This information can help her pick up the pace and get more done.

Summarize Results

After you have completed your time log each day, go back, highlight, and summarize your results.

Red: Highlight[*] in red the Time Bandits[**] and items you want to avoid, delegate, or perform more effectively.

Green: Next, highlight[*] in green the items where you were effectively spending time on activities that were important to you.

Circles mean chunks[***]: Then circle the entries where you spent a one-hour or greater uninterrupted "chunk of time" on important activities and priorities.

---

[*] Use pale or pastel highlighters so you can see what you highlight; alternatively, underline items in red and green instead of highlighting.

[**] We discuss *Time Bandits* and techniques for dealing with them in *Step 4: Make Each Day Count.*

[***] For a definition of a chunk of time see *Chunk Your Time* in *Step 4, Make Each Day Count.*

Make Changes

NOW THAT you have highlighted and circled the entries on your time log, it is time to find obstacles and opportunities where you can make changes.

Eliminate red: Look at each red item and ask yourself what you can do to eliminate or avoid it. If you cannot eliminate or avoid the red items, can you bunch them up and get them all done at once? An example is responding to non-critical mail and email at set times rather than continuously throughout the day.

Replicate green: Review your green items, where you spent your time effectively. Reflect on the steps you took to be effective and see if you can identify any good strategies or techniques that you can use again.

Increase circles: Look over your time log to find opportunities where you could have eliminated interruptions, stops, and starts to create more one-hour uninterrupted chunks of time on your green activities. Make a note of the techniques you could have used and start using them. The more circles you have in a day, the better.

Take action to make changes: Now that you know what to do, make decisions and commit to the specific actions you will take and changes you will make to manage your time better. Record these in your journal.

Dos and Don'ts

Do:

- Try time logs. Select a minimum of two to three days and keep a time log.
- Use the time log technique once each quarter, and periodically as needed to stay focused, eliminate time bandits, streamline your days, and be in control.

Don't:

- Fool yourself by thinking you can manage your time without first knowing how you are spending your time now, because you cannot.

Think of your plan for the week ahead
as an advance copy of the pages from
your book of life.

—Jim Ball

You must give some time to your fellow
man. Even if it's a little thing, do some-
thing for those who have need of help,
something for which you get no pay but
the privilege of doing it. For remember,
you don't live in a world all your own.
Your brothers are here, too.

—Albert Schweitzer

Step 3:
Plan Your Weeks

Weekly Planners Achieve More

ONE OF the most profound observations we have made over the years is that only a small percentage of people plan their weeks in a deliberate and systematic manner.

While many people think through a daily plan, very few people begin their weeks with a solid plan.

This observation is important because individuals who deliberately and systematically plan their weeks accomplish much more than those who do not!

Most people begin their week with only a general idea of what they are going to do. They do not begin Monday morning with definite goals that they intend to accomplish during the week and definite plans for achieving them.

This is because people often have a passive mentality and do not understand the value of a week. They do not see themselves as being in control. They do not visualize and assertively pursue what they want to achieve. Instead, they "handle things." They accept their weeks as they come. Day-by-day they react to whatever occurs.

Sadly, these individuals do not understand the value of time. They believe they have more time than they do.

If you are serious about achieving your potential and managing your time well, then you must be proactive. Weekly planning is a must.

Adopt a Weekly Planning Habit

OUR RECOMMENDATION is that you adopt a lifetime habit where you prepare a **weekly plan** each week for the upcoming week.

It is best to prepare your weekly plan at the same time and place each week to reinforce the habit.

Many people, and we are included, do their weekly planning in their offices. People who do not have an office often plan their weeks at home sitting at the kitchen table or in a study. Pick a time and place that works for you and stick with it.

Get Some Quiet Time

We need to slow down and give our brains a few minutes to settle and clear out our thoughts of the day before we can do a good job of planning the days ahead.

In preparation for planning your week ahead, clear off your desk, file your papers away, and go where others will not interrupt you. If you do not have an office, find some place where you will not be disturbed for a few minutes and where you can reflect and think.

Plan Your Weeks on Friday

FOR PEOPLE who work Monday through Friday, the best day to plan your upcoming week is Friday. There are four reasons why you should plan on Friday.

Reason #1—Jumpstart Monday: You have a better chance of having a full and productive week if you begin strong than if you do not. It is therefore important to come into Monday morning fully charged, raring to go, and knowing exactly what you intend to do.

Reason #2—Team coordination: If you are working with others and prepare your plan on Friday, you have the opportunity to coordinate with them. That way everyone can start immediately Monday morning. If you wait until Monday morning to plan your week, it will be difficult for everyone to get off to a great start.

Reason #3—Subconscious auto-guidance: When you prepare your weekly plan on Friday, without any additional effort on your part, you will work your plan in your mind over the weekend. As a result, you will enter Monday prepared to achieve what you were subconsciously thinking about over the weekend.

Reason #4—Timely use of feedback: By preparing your weekly plan on Friday, you can reflect back to see how well you did during the week. This provides timely feedback that you can use to adjust your thoughts and make changes to be more effective the following week.

It's About TIME!

Paul's Experience

JIM HAS a friend, Paul, who is also a client. Jim has coached and worked with Paul for several years to help him achieve his potential and his dreams. Paul is extremely successful.

Paul was a Monday morning planner: When Jim started working with Paul, Jim asked Paul to send us a weekly plan using the format and approach we use. Jim also asked Paul to do this on Friday.

Paul saw the value in preparing a weekly plan, but he did not want to do it on Fridays. Paul was a Monday morning planner. Paul was used to his Monday morning routine and wanted to keep it.

Never on Monday again: After working with Paul for several months, Jim again asked Paul to try Friday afternoon for preparing his weekly plan. Paul finally agreed to try it.

"Never again…" is how Paul's email began when he transmitted his plan to Jim that first Friday. "Never again will I do my weekly plan on Monday."

By preparing his weekly plan on Friday, Paul was able to mobilize others in his office so that they could hit the ground running on Monday morning.

In addition, Paul said that his Monday morning momentum put wind in his sails to carry him through the entire week.

What is a Weekly Plan?

MANY INDIVIDUALS have told us that they plan their weeks but never write anything down.

There is no comparison between planning without writing things down and taking time to organize and record your thoughts so you can see what you are thinking.

When you write things out you force yourself to think more clearly, completely, and specifically.

Your weekly plan is not just a piece of paper. Just like a map with driving directions is a key tool for getting from point A to point B, your weekly plan **is a key tool** for establishing weekly goals and selecting specific actions **that will enable you to achieve those goals**.

Weekly Plan Format*

The format we recommend has three sections:

Goals: Enter your top goals for the week.

Days and Activities: Enter appointments and major action steps to achieve your goals.

Review and Results: Summarize your assessment of the week.

* Also, see the chapter, *The Three Magic Pieces of Paper*, where we provide an illustration of a Weekly Plan form, a recap of related preparation instructions, and information on how to download a free Weekly Plan form from The Goals Institute.

It's About TIME!

Set Your Goals for Next Week

BEGIN TO create your weekly plan by thinking through your various goals, alternatives, and priorities.

Review your top three time management goals from *Step 1* and your other personal and business goals and tasks. Then select your top one to three goals for the week and enter those on your weekly plan.

While you may have many goals of many types at any one time, we recommend focusing on one to three key goals that you intend to complete or move forward.

A huge mistake many people make is pursuing too many goals at the same time. We call this "goal clutter." People with goal clutter spin their wheels going from one goal to the other and often accomplish very little.

Thumbnail summary: Record only a thumbnail summary of each goal in your weekly plan. You do not need to write out a complete goal statement. Include the essence of the goal and its deadline.

Times and dates: Specify the *exact* deadline as to the day and time for each goal. This improves communication among team members and sets the stage for keeping a good pace and staying focused.

A goal like "complete and deliver proposal by Friday" leaves too much room for misinterpretation. A more precise goal statement would be "complete and deliver the ABC proposal by 9:00 a.m. Friday morning."

Commit to Achieving Your Goals

AFTER YOU have decided your goals for the upcoming week, read them over and make the commitment to achieve them.

Many individuals identify goals for the week, but they think of their goals as best-effort intentions. If they achieve their goals, fine, but if not, they will always be there to work on the following week.

If you really want to manage yourself and your time better, then take your weekly goals seriously. Only select goals for the week that you intend to pursue and achieve.

This is important. When people do not take their goals seriously, they get into the habit of letting their goals slide or slip by and accepting this as okay. This is a difficult habit to break and it is extremely detrimental to achieving the success you desire.

Map Out a Plan for the Week

NOW THAT you have entered your goals in your weekly plan, it is time to enter scheduled meetings, appointments, commitments, and the tasks or actions you will complete to achieve your goals for the week.

Examine each time commitment and ask yourself if it is a good investment. Is it absolutely required? Take steps to eliminate or minimize any unimportant or non-productive time commitments from your schedule.

Create a Roadmap

Create a roadmap to achieve your goals for the up-coming week by scheduling appointments or "chunks of time" in your weekly plan when you will take the actions to work toward your goals. There is a descriptive section on chunks of time in *Chunk Your Time* in *Step 4: Make Each Day Count*.

If your goal is to exercise three times a week, then schedule and enter those times in your weekly plan.

If your goal is to rehearse a presentation for two practices at one hour each, enter those hours as appointments in your weekly plan.

If your goal is to complete a report and you estimate that it will take six hours, enter those hours on your plan as a commitment. If you break this into two or three sessions, enter those times on your weekly plan.

If you have a great plan,
chances are you will have a great week.

If you have a good plan,
chances are you will have a good week.

If you have a weak plan,
chances are you will have a weak week.

If you have no plan,
chances are someone else will have your week.

—Jim Ball

Weekly Planner Options

THE THREE basic options for the type of weekly planning tools you can use are below.

Option 1: Separate Calendars and Planners

This is the approach we prefer. We use two tools. For scheduling and managing appointments, we use a spiral monthly desk calendar. For planning and managing our weekly goals and plans, we use the Weekly Plan form that is discussed and illustrated earlier and in the chapter entitled *The Three Magic Pieces of Paper*.

Option 2: Combination Calendars-Planners

Some individuals prefer a binder-based calendar-planner system. These come in various sizes and formats and contain planning pages or inserts for every day. These systems can be useful tools. A shortcoming in some of these systems is that they do not focus hard on weekly planning and daily goals. This is essential.

Option 3: Planning and Calendaring Software

The third option is to use a computer or hand-held data device with software for calendaring and goal and action planning. These options are fine, too, as long as you supplement them as needed to apply the fundamental principles and strategies described herein.

Review and Learn

YOUR WEEKLY PLAN provides a foundation for evaluating how well you are doing.

Spend a few minutes at the end of each week reviewing your plan and results for the past week. Here are some questions to consider:

- What worked well and what did not work well?
- Was it a good week or a great week?
- Did you make good investments of your time?
- Were you in control? If not, what were the obstacles and how can you eliminate them?
- What are your habits for managing yourself? Are they what you want them to be?
- How did you do at achieving your goals for the week? What could you have done differently?

Jot down a short evaluation of the week in the summary part of the weekly plan form.

An example might be, "Great week! I started strong and stayed on track. I managed interruptions and spent several chunks of time on major projects. I also stuck to my schedule and got to the gym as planned."

Another example is, "Bad week. I was in damage control the whole time. Too many fires to put out. Too many interruptions. I spent far too much time in unproductive meetings. I have got to get back on track!"

Make Changes

THE FINAL weekly planning strategy is to decide what actions, habits, routines, or patterns you will work on or change during your week to manage your time better.

Do not skip this step.

Spend a few minutes reviewing your weekly plan and results. Identify and think through specific strategies and actions to improve. Pay particular attention to actions you must take to acquire or reinforce the good time management habits you want to adopt.

Write your strategies and actions in your journal and incorporate these into your weekly plan for the next week. Then implement them.

If you do not make good or great progress in any given week, do not let it deter you or set you back. Begin fresh the following week by preparing a weekly plan.

Rosa's Story

ROSA is an experienced manager in a large quick food service business.

Although Rosa consistently has produced exceptional results at work, she told us that she was often frenzied, and she could never get everything done.

In addition, Rosa said she felt that the pressure of the time requirements of her job were negatively affecting the amount and quality of time she wanted to be spending with her daughter.

One week after using our weekly planning approach, Rosa was all smiles.

"I couldn't believe it," she said. "I wrote out my plan and got just about ninety percent of everything I wanted to accomplish at work done. That is some kind of record.

"More importantly, I spent Sunday with my little girl. I put in my plan that we would go to a movie and we did. I spent the whole day with her. Most times before I would say we would do something and then never do it.

"This weekly plan tool is great!"

Side benefit: By preparing a written plan, Rosa was able to have her area supervisor review it and provide input to help her achieve her goals for the upcoming week.

Dos and Don'ts

Do:

- Adopt the habit of preparing a weekly plan.
- Do your weekly planning at the same set time and place each week.
- Think of your weekly plan as a powerful tool for managing yourself, achieving your goals, and getting more done.
- Share your weekly plan with individuals who can provide feedback to improve your plan or help you achieve your goals.

Don't:

- Think you can do a good job of planning your weeks without writing your plans down.
- Start your week without first deciding what you really want to accomplish during the week.

One of the illusions in life is that the present hour is not the decisive, critical hour. Write it on your heart that today is the best day of your life.

—Ralph Waldo Emerson

Somebody ought to tell us, right at the start of our lives, that we are dying. Then we might live life to the limit every minute of the day. Do it, I say, whatever you want to do, do it now.

—Michael Landon

Mr. Landon, "Little" Joe in the television series Bonanza, knew he was dying at the time. He died at age 54.

Step 4:
Make Each Day Count

The Most Important Progress to Make

MANY PEOPLE get up and begin each day with an attitude of, "Here I am day, take me."

The problem with this approach is that the day *will* take you. Someone or some event will come along and suck up every single minute you have, if you let them.

And *that* you must not do. You must not let others control your time or your destiny.

You must enter the day and take it.

The most important progress to make in life is *daily progress*. If you take care of making daily progress toward your desired goals and results, your weeks and years will take care of themselves.

However, if you allow a day to pass by without being productive, soon one day becomes two. Two days slip to three. Before you know it, weeks and years will pass and your once exciting hopes and dreams will fade into distant memories never to be achieved.

Do you *really* want to manage your time, be effective, have more flexibility in your schedule, and get more done while enjoying life more? If you do, then focus hard on making each of your days the best day you can possibly make it.

To do that, enter each day with a plan.

Start Each Day with a List of Thunderbolts[*]

A THUNDERBOLT in nature is a huge bolt of lightning with a loud clap of thunder. It is a powerful force.

Jim coined the term *Thunderbolt* to refer to the **five most important goals** that you intend to accomplish during a given day.

Although he did not call them Thunderbolts initially, Jim first learned about the Thunderbolt technique when he read about it years ago.

A man told Andrew Carnegie, the industrialist, to write down his five most important items for the next day and then come in the next day and work his list in priority order.

As the story goes, Carnegie followed the man's advice. Shortly thereafter Carnegie wrote the man a check for $25,000 because he felt the technique the man had suggested was so valuable!

If Carnegie were around to make an equivalent payment today, the amount would be in the millions.

Would you like to benefit from advice worth millions of dollars? Read on.

* Also, see the chapter, *The Three Magic Pieces of Paper*, where we provide an illustration of a Thunderbolt Card form, a recap of related preparation instructions, and information on how to download a free Thunderbolt Card form from The Goals Institute.

What Is a Thunderbolt?

LET US FIRST clarify that Thunderbolts are not "to do" items, which we discuss later, and they are not actions or activities that you list to map out or fill up your day.

A Thunderbolt is a substantive goal that you want to achieve and intend to achieve in its entirety during the day.

A Thunderbolt can be two types of goals. It can be an end-result goal or it can be a supporting goal such as an interim milestone or action step that will cause or help cause an end-result goal to be attained.

An example of a Thunderbolt that is an end-result goal is completing an important report or paper. An example of a Thunderbolt that is a supporting goal is completing ten calls to gather information for the report.

Five Item Limit

Your Thunderbolt list should be no more than five items long. It can be fewer than five items, but not more.

When people add more than five items to their Thunderbolt list, they jeopardize the whole list. More items tend to overwhelm people. They go back and forth, procrastinate, and do a little bit here and there.

When people have only five major items to deal with, they are energized. They start work immediately, stay focused and on track, and get results.

Thunderbolts Are Different

THERE ARE several key points we want you to know about Thunderbolts.

First, Thunderbolts are substantive goals that are important and significant to you.

Many people approach each day as though the objective is to schedule out existing tasks to fill the day. They begin planning their days with questions like: What can I do with my time? What projects should I work on?

A person with a Thunderbolt approach begins each day with a different objective. Rather than trying to fill their days with existing tasks, they begin by first reflecting on the important longer-term personal, career, business, and other goals they want to achieve.

To plan your days with Thunderbolts, start by answering two questions different from those above: "What am I trying to accomplish?" "What must I do to achieve that?"

Second, Thunderbolts are not vague or possible goals that you are considering. Thunderbolts are definite choices about specific goals for the day.

Third, Thunderbolts are not goals you will work on or give your best efforts to during the day. Thunderbolts are specific results you intend to accomplish or complete some time before the end of the day.

The Power of Thunderbolts

THUNDERBOLTS ARE powerful because they force us to create a written plan for the day that focuses on a small number of important tasks.

By prioritizing and investing time on what is important, non-productive and unimportant items tend to disappear from the day or the time spent on them is kept to only what is essential.

When we begin our day with a Thunderbolt list, we have a mission to accomplish. We have power and conviction. This makes it easier to fend off interruptions and stay on track.

If you go into work in the morning with a list of meaty items to accomplish during the day and someone asks you if you have five minutes, you can honestly say, "I'm sorry, but I have a lot to get done today. Can I catch you maybe at the end of the day or over lunch?"

This strong start can create enough momentum to carry you through the entire day.

However, if you enter your day without a list of goals you intend to accomplish, you are vulnerable. Without a plan, when someone asks you if you have five minutes, you are more likely to say yes than no. This weak start can carry over to the entire day.

Prepare Tomorrow's Thunderbolts Today

IN ORDER for Thunderbolts to be effective in helping you manage your time better, you must prepare your Thunderbolts for tomorrow before you end today.

Many people have told us that they like to plan their day in the morning before they do anything else. This is not as effective or as powerful as planning your day the day before. There are several reasons for this.

Reason #1—Jumpstart your day: We all have a better chance of having a productive day if we begin strong. A slow start in the morning can wreck an entire day. However, if we start strong and productive, this momentum can build and carry us through the day.

Reason #2—Team coordination: If you are working with others and plan tomorrow before you leave today, you have the opportunity to coordinate with them and delegate tasks before they leave for the day. This way everyone can start immediately in the morning.

Reason #3—Subconscious auto-guidance: By preparing your Thunderbolts the day before you intend to implement them you will subconsciously work your plan in your mind through the night. As a result, you will wake up in the morning cued to go. You will enter the morning keenly aware of what you were subconsciously thinking about all night long.

How to Prepare a Thunderbolts List In 5 Steps

PREPARE a daily Thunderbolt list by following the five "ize" steps below:

1. Journalize

Take a few minutes to think about tomorrow. Jot down on a note pad the important goals you want to accomplish. Then select the five (5) goals that are the most important for tomorrow and enter these on your Thunderbolt card. These are your Thunderbolts.

2. Prioritize

Review your five Thunderbolts and prioritize them. Although all goals may be important, rank the relative importance of them from one to five, with one being the most important and five being the least important.

3. Visualize

Before leaving work and again just before retiring for the evening, spend a few moments visualizing yourself completing each of your Thunderbolts. You do not have to spend a lot of time doing this. A couple of minutes will do. Just close your eyes and see yourself taking action and accomplishing each Thunderbolt.

4. Initialize

Begin immediately the next morning by working on your number one Thunderbolt first. Do this as soon as you get to work. Do not allow any distractions before you start. Continue working on your first item in a concentrated manner until it is finished or completed as far as you can take it for the day.

5. Finalize

After you have completed the first Thunderbolt or pushed it as far as you can, move on to the second one. Repeat this process until you finalize all the Thunderbolts that you can. Cross Thunderbolts off your list when you complete them. Concentrate on a single task until you finish it. Avoid drabs, dribbles, and starting many tasks at the same time.

Get Into a Thunderbolt Habit

Like brushing your teeth, **Thunderbolts must become a daily habit to produce lasting results**.

Most people are in the habit of starting their days with a list of to do items. While this is a good habit for being organized, the to do list habit that most people have is quite different from a Thunderbolt approach.

Exchanging your current habit for a daily Thunderbolt habit may take time and persistence because it is a new way of approaching the day. The long-term and lifetime results will be worth the effort.

Special Thunderbolt Tips

BELOW ARE several additional tips, techniques, and suggestions for getting the maximum benefits from using Thunderbolts to plan and manage your days.

Handling Interruptions

There will be times when you cannot start working on your Thunderbolts first thing in the morning and there will be times when you are interrupted and cannot work your Thunderbolt plan the way you intended.

If **required** and **unavoidable** events prevent you from working your Thunderbolt list first thing in the morning, or if important and unplanned events interrupt your flow during the day, then do what you must do to address those circumstances and needs.

As soon as the event is over, go back to your Thunderbolt list and start anew on the item you were working on before the interruption.

Press Yourself

One of the best pieces of advice we can provide to help you increase your lifelong achievements is this: *Really* press yourself to accomplish as much as you possibly can each day.

Think big: When you set your Thunderbolts for a day, do not just list the results you can achieve with

It's About TIME!

ease. Raise your sights and establish stretch Thunderbolts that will cause you to grow and achieve your potential.

Be firm. When you set your Thunderbolts for a day, stick to them and achieve them.

Evaluate and keep score: At the end of each day, evaluate how well you did at achieving your Thunderbolts. Take any appropriate actions to do better tomorrow. Also, set up measurements to check how much work you completed today and take steps to complete more tomorrow.

Get as much done as you can: Many people put in long hours, but only a small percentage of people try to get as much done as possible in the hours available.

Work, meetings, and activities fill the time available. Because we know we will be back at work tomorrow, we leave some of today's work for tomorrow.

We do not recommend that you press so hard during the day that you stress yourself out and come to the verge of a breaking point.

However, we do recommend that you pick up the pace when you can and make each day as productive as possible. If you accomplish just a little more each day, the long-term impact will be enormous.

This is a cliché, but it is good advice: *Do not put off until tomorrow what you can complete today.*

Keep Thunderbolts Visible

To get the greatest value from the Thunderbolt technique, keep your list visible on your desk or in eyesight during the day. This will serve as a reminder during the day and help you focus and work your plan.

People use a variety of techniques to keep their Thunderbolt lists visible during the day. Some individuals tape their Thunderbolts to a wall or their computer monitor. Some put them on a bulletin board. Others put them in a special holder on their desk.

Do whatever works for you, but keep your Thunderbolt list in eyesight so you are continually aware of your plans for the day and can get back on track quickly if you get distracted.

Thunderbolts Are Great Motivators

A great benefit of Thunderbolts is how motivating they are. When individuals focus on one item, complete it, and cross it off their list, they feel in control and have a genuine sense of accomplishment.

"I used to feel like I was being picked to death by sparrows," a client told us when she described how she tried to work her long list of to do items each day. "With Thunderbolts, a big weight has been lifted off my shoulders. They are so liberating!"

Using Thunderbolts to Acquire New Habits

Thunderbolts are helpful tools to use when you are acquiring new habits or skills.

For example, perhaps you are starting a new exercise program and going to the gym is a high priority for you. In this case, "Get to the gym after work" is a Thunderbolt. You may want to enter "Get to the gym after work" on your Thunderbolt list for a few days or even weeks until you get into the habit of going to the gym.

Once you are in a routine of going to the gym, you no longer need to record the action as a Thunderbolt.

Our Special Technique for Achieving Goals

A special technique we recommend is to look over your Thunderbolt list after you have prepared it and highlight those items that relate to the major long-term goals that you are pursuing currently.

If you do not find a Thunderbolt to highlight, you are not going to be making progress tomorrow on your major lifetime goals. If not, your goals for the day are not aligned with and supporting your long-term goals. You may want to rethink your Thunderbolts.

Highlighting daily Thunderbolts that relate to your major lifetime goals is a simple, easy step that can help you stay on track to your major goals. It also can help you avoid fooling yourself that you are making progress when in reality your long-term goals may be slipping away.

Chunk Your Time

JIM FIRST HEARD the word "chunk" used in reference to time years ago when he saw the previously mentioned Peter Drucker training tape on time management.

In his book *Managing for Results*, Drucker wrote, "Concentration is the most frequently violated principle in business. We seem intent on spending our time in drabs and dribbles trying to do a little bit of everything rather than concentrating our resources on the primary tasks at hand."

To avoid this dilution of efforts, Drucker recommends that we spend our time in *chunks*.

Valuable advice: Aside from having a goal in the first place, and making sure it is the right goal, Drucker's recommendation to spend time in chunks is the most important advice we have ever received or come across for managing our personal effectiveness and for achieving our business and personal goals.

What Is a "Chunk?"

A chunk of time is a minimum of **one-hour**, **uninterrupted**. A one-hour segment is special.

An hour seems to be the minimum time necessary to reach our more creative thoughts. Our mind takes several minutes to clear before we focus. Then once we are focused, we do not get into our deeper, more powerful thoughts for several more minutes. By investing an uninterrupted hour, we go deeper and engage the best and most creative parts of our minds.

It is the same with physical work and skills development. It takes time to get started, reach our stride, and attain our full physical power. By investing an uninterrupted hour, we give our bodies a chance to accomplish work and learn skills at top performing levels.

In addition to helping us reach the peaks of our mental and physical abilities, the chunking time technique produces the power of concentration because it crowds out interruptions and energy losses from stops and starts.

Note that chunks of time must be **uninterrupted**. Even the slightest interruption can break your power of concentration. Once a break occurs, you may never regain a great thought or reach a new level of physical skill you were on the verge of achieving.

A one-hour chunk does not have to be spent alone. You can chunk time with others when you are working together on projects.

The Importance of Chunks

Chunking time produces exceptional results.

By spending an hour of concentrated thinking or effort on a matter, you have the opportunity to achieve breakthrough results.

No one, not even the great geniuses of all time, has had breakthrough ideas without applying concentrated periods of thought. Although a breakthrough or revelation may appear to pop out in a momentary flash, it was the hours of concentrated preparation that forced the idea to the surface.

Similarly, by spending an hour of concentrated physical effort on one activity you give yourself a chance to practice, learn, and acquire skill. No one ever became a great pianist or a gold-medal athlete by practicing in fifteen-minute spurts. Extended periods of practice are required.

> *I could never have done what I have done . . . without the determination to concentrate myself on one project at a time.*
>
> —Charles Dickens

How to Chunk Time

The best way to chunk your time is to schedule your time in chunks and take action to enforce the schedule.

Plan chunks weekly: When you are creating your weekly plan, identify several chunks during the week when you can focus and get results. Put these chunks on your calendar as appointments. Keep them in mind as things come up during the week, and protect them from interruptions and diversions.

Plan chunks daily: When you prepare your Thunderbolts for the next day, set aside specific times during the day when you intend to chunk your time on specific Thunderbolts. Try to identify any possible obstacles to your chunking and take steps to avoid them.

Create chunking strategies: When it is time to chunk your time, let co-workers know that you do not want to be disturbed for an hour. Tell them you will be working on something important and ask their help not to be disturbed. Turn off your cell phone and computer. If you will be using your computer for your chunk, turn off the email system so you will not get email.

Aim for at least a chunk or two a day: It usually is not possible or desirable to spend your whole day going from one chunk activity to another chunk activity all day long with no breaks in between.

We recommend that you try to get in two or more chunks a day, if possible. One chunk in the morning and one in the afternoon would be a good start.

If this is not possible and all you can get in is one chunk a day or one chunk every other day, then start with that and do what you can.

Getting Creative to
Chunk Your Time

IF YOU are in a situation at work where you are the point person for others to contact or where you provide support for others, it may be hard for you to chunk time during the normal workday. However, it is not impossible.

Sometimes you have to get creative.

Cyndi, an administrative assistant to three executives, told us during a seminar that our chunking time technique would not work for her. She said she was responsible for helping too many people and there was no way she could carve out a one-hour chunk, "even though that would be great."

When we pursued this with Cyndi, we suggested she discuss the chunking concept with the executives she worked with and see if they had any ideas.

Cyndi called us shortly after the seminar. To her surprise, the executives she worked with thought time chunking for Cyndi was a great idea. They worked with Cyndi to help her schedule at least one hour a day to work on her priority projects.

"It doesn't always work out every single day," Cyndi said. "But I do get in three or four chunks every week."

Investing Your Chunks of Time

WHEN YOU schedule a chunk of time, make sure you have a goal for what you want to accomplish. Below are four areas where time chunking provides great benefits.

Goals and Priorities

Chunk time on top priorities, critical matters, and re-sults-producing actions that relate to your most important goals at work or at home.

Growth and Development

Chunk time on activities that will help you improve the knowledge, skills, and abilities that are important to your career and personal growth.

Building Relationships at Work

Chunk time on activities that will enhance your relationships with associates at work. One of the best chunks of time you can invest is time with another associate where you plan your work together and share ideas.

Family and Friends

Perhaps the best way to spend time with family members and friends is to do it in chunks. We recommend that you chunk your time with family members, friends, those in need, and others who you care about.

Jim's Chunking Time Story

A NUMBER of years ago a friend asked if I chunked my time with my family.

I said yes.

My friend pressed me. He said, "When was the last time you spent a one-hour uninterrupted chunk with your daughter, Stephanie?"

That put me on the spot. Stephanie was twelve and I tried to remember the last time we had a one-hour chunk of time together, just Stephanie and me. I recalled many times together as a family, but I could not remember a single time when Stephanie and I were alone.

That night at dinner, I announced to Stephanie that I wanted to spend an hour or so with her, just her and me, alone. Stephanie stopped in her tracks.

"Why?" Stephanie asked. She looked at Jennifer, her older sister, for guidance. Jennifer shrugged her shoulders. I am sure Jennifer was silently hoping she would not be next.

I told Stephanie that I just wanted to spend an hour alone with her.

"What would we do?" Stephanie asked.

We agreed to a dinner date and decided to make it special, at a fancy restaurant. My wife, Dolly, took Stephanie shopping for a new dress.

It's About TIME!

I cannot adequately explain exactly what happened the evening of our dinner date. However, I can tell you that it changed the relationship between Stephanie and me forever. I went into that restaurant with one daughter and came out with one I had never quite known before.

That night we chunked time together for several hours. We shut out the rest of the world and just talked. In the process, we had a bonding that I cannot describe. The whole evening was wonderful.

This "experiment" was so successful and rewarding that I began repeating my time-chunking dates with Stephanie, and with my daughter, Jennifer. There were times when Stephanie was in high school when she would ask if I would like to have a chunk with her, "say Thursday at noon."

I'd smile and agree. On Thursday, I would write her a note to take to school: "Please excuse Stephanie from school today at noon; she has an appointment."

The appointment was with me, for lunch. We were chunking.

I have made chunking time with my daughters and my wife a ritual in my life. It is one of the best habits I have ever acquired.

If you have never chunked time with those you love and care about, try it. It can change your life, and their lives, too!

Time Bandit Robbery

"CAN I have five minutes?"

What do you say when asked that question?

Most people say yes.

Wrong answer: Saying yes usually is the wrong answer when you want to manage your time better.

To begin with, five minutes is *never* five minutes.

In addition to the true time loss itself, whatever it may be, a yes answer can cause several problems.

If you say yes, you subconsciously program yourself to undervalue your time and overvalue the time of others. One yes can lead to many yeses.

A yes answer also is a signal to yourself that you have all the time in the world. This is not correct. Your time is finite. Remember the sand in the hourglass.

The biggest cost: When you say yes and allow a five-minute interruption, the biggest cost often is your break in concentration on what you were doing.

You lose mental momentum.

You also can lose the possibility of idea breakthroughs that may have been just moments away. You may never regain the valuable and important thoughts you were on the verge of formulating. This occurs more often than people imagine and the cost to you over your lifetime is tremendous.

When and How to Say No

RATHER THAN adopting a soft line and always saying yes, or a hard line and always saying no, we recommend a three-stage approach to five-minute requests of your time. This approach only takes a few moments to apply.

First, assess the importance and urgency of what you are doing. **Second**, assess who is making the request and your best guess of the importance and urgency of the request to them. **Third**, manage the interruption by either deferring it or by saying no immediately.

Deferring is easy: Unless the five-minute request is from a superior, an authoritative person, someone in an emergency situation or in great need, your mother, spouse, or one of your kids, it is usually easy to quickly defer the request to another time.

Just say something like, "I am really busy on an important task right now, can I call you this afternoon?"

Saying no: Saying no is harder, but it often is the best answer. For a no, you could say something like, "I'm sorry, I really don't have the time; could you get someone else to help you?"

If an individual persists, you may have to become firmer. Once you decide to say no, you must stick to it because the moment you show a sign of weakening the other person will persist even more.

Other Time Bandits to Avoid

IN ADDITION to saying no to routine interruptions that we can avoid, we must also learn to say no to Time Bandits that steal and squander our time in other ways.

Say no to too much television: Mindless, content-free television watching is the worst Time Bandit for many people.

Statistics vary depending upon who provides them, but many studies report that the average person watches 20 to 25 hours of television a week. That is a lot of television. More importantly, it is a lot of your life.

If you watch an average of 22 hours of television per week, this is one-fifth of the waking time in your life!

We enjoy television and sometimes watch a mindless, content-free program like most people do. However, we try to limit our television time to those programs or events that are worth our time investment.

For example, instead of watching television at night, for the past few weeks we have spent many of our evening hours writing this book. We would rather be able to have this book completed and in your hands than be able to say we watched 200 additional hours of television.

Say no to too much time on the Internet: Some time spent on the Internet can be productive, but too much can be a Time Bandit just like television.

Say no to news, information, and media overload:
A huge Time Bandit can be the collective information
we receive and the time we spend processing it.

Every newspaper we get, every magazine we subscribe to, every piece of mail we open, and every time
we turn on the news causes us to spend time processing
information.

While it is important to learn and stay current, it is
not necessary to be up to the minute on everything.

Unless you are in the information business, you do
not have to watch the morning, midday, evening, and
late-night news to be informed. If a new continent is discovered, someone will tell you!

Try this for magazines: We subscribe to many
magazines related to our business, and it would take
hours and hours to read them all from cover to cover.
We therefore peruse the table of contents and then read
only those articles that are important or are of immediate
interest. We may miss a few items with this approach,
however, we minimize the time we spend with portions
of magazines that have a low time-to-value payback.

> *I do not take a single newspaper, nor
> read one a month, and I feel myself infi-
> nitely the happier for it.*
>
> —Thomas Jefferson

Say no to organizations and events that are not important to you: Every commitment you make by joining an organization or being on a civic or neighborhood committee and every invitation you accept will spend your time for you.

It can be a tough choice to drop out of a group or decline an invitation. However, sometimes you must make tough choices like these if you want to control your time and your life and achieve your goals.

As Charles Darwin said, "A man who dares waste one hour of life has not discovered the value of life."

Think Longer Term

It is important to have a long-term perspective when you make choices about how you will spend your time. Rather than making short-term-only decisions, take a moment to decide the best choice for you in terms of the longer-term results you desire.

If someone pleads with you to go to a movie, but on a longer-term basis you know you would be better off going to the gym to stay on your fitness program, then say no. This is a clear example of how your power of choice can and will shape your life, and your body, too.

One of the worst trade-offs people make is forgoing longer-term lasting achievements and results for short-term passing pleasures.

Individuals who have tremendous lifetime successes also make many short-term sacrifices.

Sometimes It Is
Hard to Say No

YEARS AGO, Jim was on track to become president of a local community organization. At the time, he also was starting his first business, a venture capital firm.

After thinking through his goals and plans, Jim concluded he did not have time to do both tasks well.

While Jim did not like having to tell the board of the community organization that he was stepping out of the presidential cue, he did so to make sure he could launch his business successfully. Several board members were vocally upset with Jim. They got together as a group and tried to persuade him to stay on. He said no.

After Jim's new venture was well underway, Jim recommitted himself to community efforts. He co-founded and was the first president of the George Mason University Century Club, an organization that supports entrepreneurial endeavors and the university. That organization is still going strong.

The point is, Jim recognized when he did not have enough time to do everything well. In order to invest his time in his business, Jim had to make choices about when he would participate in community affairs.

Get Yourself a Hideaway

OVER THE YEARS, we have observed that everyone who gets a lot done has a hideaway.

When we say hideaway, we mean exactly that, some place where you can hide and get away from everything that is a distraction to your thoughts and concentration.

We are plugged in everywhere—by cell phone, telephone, e-mail, and voice mail. Advertisers want our attention and our time and they continually bombard us with information and interruptions.

No one can unplug totally from the world, and we are not recommending that you try.

What we are recommending is that you disconnect from everyone and everything periodically so you can reconnect with yourself and concentrate on what you want to accomplish.

It is important to pause and look inward to your thoughts. It is also important to concentrate and focus your efforts when you have an important task or project you want to complete.

Many individuals do not spend a single hour a month in quiet time with themselves.

They should.

Examples of Hideaways

A hideaway is any place you can unplug and retreat from your busy world.

Many writers, for example, are productive only when they have a special place to concentrate. In his book, *On Writing*, Stephen King describes how he has a special room where he goes to write undisturbed. Danielle Steele has a separate residence for her writing.

A separate room or residence might be great if you could arrange them, however where you go to get away is not as important as unplugging from distractions.

One of Jennifer's favorite hideaways is in the lobby of big hotels when she is traveling. Many people go by, but Jennifer is not plugged into them so she can concentrate uninterrupted on her thoughts.

Jim's favorite hideaways for writing are airplanes or trains when he is traveling, and the beach when he takes a few days off. Even though many people are around, Jim is not connected to them so he can hide away from his regular world, think, and write.

For his hideaway, one individual we know has a breakfast meeting at the same hotel every morning around seven. What is neat about this is that most of the time he is meeting only with himself!

Try the Five O'clock Club

WE KNOW a number of executives who go to work early in the morning so that they can be alone and get something done before everyone else arrives.

Mary Kay Ash, the founder of Mary Kay, Inc., wrote about using this early morning technique in her book, *Mary Kay*.

For her hideaway, she formed the Five O'clock Club. Ash explained that three early risings a week make an extra day in the week.

She wrote, "If I get up at five o'clock for three mornings, I'll have an eight-day week. That's what I've been looking for!"

Although Ms. Ash has passed on, before she left she provided good advice about hideaways to her associates and others.

If you would like an extra productivity boost several days a week, try her Five O'clock Club. To join, just get up and get going at five in the morning!

> *It is an experiment worth trying to be alone and quiet for a brief period every day.*

—Richard J. McCracken

Dos and Don'ts

Do:

- Treat each day as a gift and enter the day committed to achieving as much as you can.
- Get into the lifelong habit of planning your days with Thunderbolts.
- Chunk your time. Make appointments with yourself and others to spend your time in uninterrupted chunks of one hour or more.
- Learn to say no.
- Create or find a hideaway and use it.

Don't:

- Let people, events, or circumstances control your time.
- Expect to acquire all the techniques in this chapter overnight. Although the techniques are simple and easy, it takes time to work with them and make them your own.

Be systematic. A person who does business by rule, having a time and place for everything, doing his work promptly, will accomplish twice as much and with half the trouble of a person who does it carelessly and slipshod.

—P.T. Barnum

Step 5:
Work Smarter

Be Systematic

ONE OF the key attributes that separates highly effective people from those who are not is that highly effective people are *systematic*.

Highly effective people have routines, rituals, and processes that guide everything they do.

> *Almost all men are intelligent; it is method that they lack.*
>
> —F. W. Nichol

Slow Down to Speed Up

In order to speed up, we must first learn how to slow down. We need to slow down so that we can evaluate how we are doing what we are doing and find ways to improve the methods and techniques we are using.

Most people are so busy working on their work they do not take time to work *on the way they do their work*.

This is more than just taking time to sharpen the saw so we can cut more wood in less time with less effort. It is also about taking time to find a better or more powerful saw. In addition, it is about taking time to discover or create new ways for cutting wood—perhaps with laser-directed robotic saws.

If you want to work smarter, **first think smarter**.

Create Tools and Processes

TO START being more systematic, first analyze your work, identify the repeatable tasks you perform, and improve the tools and techniques you use to perform them.

This is an important concept that many people fail to understand or employ. The examples that follow illustrate what we mean.

Sales professional: Rob is a sales professional who spends time on the road calling on new accounts. When he returns to his office, Rob types the contact information into his contact management system and writes letters thanking his prospective customers for their time.

After Rob learned about creating tools for his repeatable processes, he invested in a device that reads the business cards he collects into his system so he does not have to spend time typing them. In addition, instead of creating a new letter for each contact, Rob created six template letters that he uses for all contacts.

Rob saved time by stopping to create tools for his repeatable processes. The techniques Rob employed are not huge innovations. They are small steps that save a few minutes each time he processes a new prospect.

Technology leader: Ruby leads a group of professionals who respond to questions users have about her company's software.

After Ruby focused on creating tools for repeatable processes she discovered that her team answered a small number of questions repeatedly.

To reduce the time required for these common questions, Ruby asked her team to create a web page that answered the 25 most frequently asked questions. She then made users aware of these questions on her company's website. The number of calls dropped substantially.

Ruby and her team saved time by stopping to create tools for their repeatable processes.

Customer service training: Julie provides orientation training for all of the new customer service agents her company hires. Historically Julie trained several people each week on each new employee's start day.

After Julie learned about creating tools for her repeatable processes, she did two things.

First, she had someone videotape about an hour of her presentations. She used this videotape in her training program so she would not have to be present when new employees learned routine information.

Second, she worked with people in the human resources department to schedule all new hires to start on Mondays. This way she could schedule the training to take place only once a week.

In addition, the individuals in the human resources department found that it also is quicker for them to process all new hires on the same day.

Look at Your Work Flow

A GOOD APPROACH to becoming more systematic is to take a visual look at your workflow and see what steps you can eliminate, combine, rearrange, or improve.

First, create a flowchart of the steps you currently take to accomplish your primary tasks. Lay out your flowchart in a time-sequenced manner, from left to right. For each step, enter a box on the chart with a description of the action. Connect the steps with lines and arrows to show the flow and interrelationships among the steps.

Next, review your flowchart to identify steps you can eliminate or combine to save time. Look at the flow to identify opportunities for rearranging steps to avoid duplicate work or speed things up. Think about how you can create tools or approaches to simplify your work. Ask others to make suggestions for improvement.

Flowcharts often reveal opportunities for handling work in a batch.

Kirby, a computer services salesman, looked at his workflow and found he could save time by preparing all of his follow-up letters and packages at the end of the day rather than completing them one-by-one during the day as he made calls.

For some people this simple technique may seem obvious. It was not obvious to Kirby, however, until he took time to reflect on how he was doing his work.

Begin with a Strong,
Bold First Step

AN EASY technique to adopt for working smarter is also a great technique for improving your overall effectiveness and results. Here it is.

Begin everything with a strong, bold first step.

People who put in an enthusiastic effort at the beginning are more likely to end strong and with success than those who have weak or half-hearted beginnings.

This applies to the beginning of everything.

Start each of your months, weeks, and days with a strong and bold first step.

Start each new project, task, or assignment with a strong and bold first step.

Start each meeting with a strong and bold first step.

Simplify

TWO OF THE GREATEST obstacles to success in managing our time well are quantity and complexity.

We have too many variables, too many selections, and too many demands upon our time.

Sometimes our work and personal lives silently, slowly, and invisibly evolve into something like an overcrowded garden where rampant weeds have taken over and are choking out the plants.

Once a garden is overgrown, the way to fix it is to pull out the weeds, prune the plants, and start fresh. Then after the garden is replanted, you must continue weeding the weeds and paring the plants. If you do not, soon you will be right back where you started.

We are the same. Over time, our lives at home and our jobs at work will become overcrowded, entangled, and unwieldy. We must periodically take time to cut back and eliminate. We must simplify and start fresh.

> *Simplicity, simplicity, simplicity. I say,*
> *let your affairs be as two or three, and*
> *not a hundred or a thousand; instead*
> *of a million count a half a dozen, and*
> *keep your accounts on your thumbnail.*
> *Simplify, simplify . . .*

—Henry David Thoreau

Eliminate Clutter

THERE IS a name for the weeds in our lives. It is clutter.

Clutter chokes us, drags us down, and sucks up the energy and drive in our lives. If we are going to be nimble in managing our time and getting things done, we must keep clutter out of our lives.

Goal Clutter

Goal clutter exists when we have too many goals to deal with at any one time.

When we are trapped in goal clutter, instead of focusing on completing a small number of goals, we spend time going back and forth, switching from goal to goal.

To eliminate goal clutter, first organize and prioritize your goals. Then select one to three significant goals to pursue. Focus only on those until they are achieved or well underway before pursuing any additional goals.

Physical Clutter

Physical clutter is all the knickknacks, magazines, books, papers, clothes, furniture, computer files, and other "stuff" you have around your office or home.

Clutter is a brain drain: While you may do it only subconsciously, you continuously look at every knickknack, magazine, book, or other piece of clutter you have. This "invisible" clutter takes real energy and mental power to process. It also distracts you.

Clutter is a physical drain: You have to deal with physical clutter physically. You have to clean it, clean around it, organize it, reorganize it, and sort through it to make choices about what to throw and where to store it.

Clutter is a money drain: It takes money to support a clutter habit. You have to buy boxes, containers, shelves, and storage devices. You may have a garage or a rental unit to store your clutter. Many people park their cars in the driveway and use their garage for their clutter. People buy clutter at garage sales and on the Internet.

Clutter is a time drain: when you have clutter, it takes time to care for it and you waste time looking through it when you should be doing important tasks.

Tips for physical clutter control: Here are several tips to consider for eliminating physical clutter.

- Open your mail by the wastebasket. Throw away junk mail without even opening it.
- Create a place for filing everything. Put everything back in its place at the end of each day.
- Clean house once a month. Go through your office and home and throw out or give away every item that you do not need or want. Start fresh and clutter-free every month.
- Get rid of knickknacks. Put them away or give them away. Better yet, do not bring them home.

We also recommend an annual "Clean Out Clutter Campaign" for every organization. One client mobilized 300 employees to clean clutter from every cubicle, room, wall, and open space. The offices looked great and everyone was energized. One manager told us people were moving and thinking faster. He said the building raised a foot up out of the ground because of the reduced weight.

Activity Clutter

Activity clutter is all of the unnecessary events, organizations, activities, and meetings that slip into our lives. Take a hard look at your calendar each month and decide which activities are and are not important. Then take steps to eliminate unimportant and nonessential activities and events from your schedule.

Information Clutter[*]

Information clutter is the raging river of unwanted and unnecessary information that pours into our lives. Information clutter is a huge problem.

Periodically step back and evaluate whether you need all the information you are getting, as often as you are getting it. Cull and pare back your sources.

Look at your magazine, newspaper, and newsletter subscriptions and weed out those that you do not need. Review your email subscriptions.

* For more ideas on dealing with information overload see *Other Time Bandits to Avoid* in *Step 4: Make Each Day Count*

How to Manage Your To Do List

MINOR TO DO items can diffuse your focus and be time wasters unless you systematically organize and process them. We recommend using a three-step approach:

1. **Adopt a single notebook system:** Record all of your To Dos in a single notebook in chronological order. Enter the date of each entry beside each To Do item. This notebook is your Master To Do list.

2. **Manage your To Dos:** Update your Master To Do list when you prepare your weekly plan.

   - Select items to act on during the week and schedule time for them in your weekly plan. Group small items into single time segments if possible.

   - Cross through items in your Master To Do list that you complete or are no longer relevant or important to you.

   - Jot down a notation as to the date you completed each item to reinforce your progress.

3. **Close out pages:** When you complete all of the items on a page in your Master To Do List, draw a diagonal line across the page to close it out.

Some people prefer to keep one notebook for personal To Dos and a second notebook for work-related To Dos. This works, too. What you want to avoid is using a variety of notepads and loose scraps of paper.

Tips for In-Box Processing

IF YOU ARE looking for a quick and easy way to be more effective and work smarter, take a look at your In Box and how you process what goes in and out of it.

Some individuals use their In Boxes more like file cabinets than they do as In Boxes.

We recommend that you set aside enough time to process incoming items and clean out your In Box completely once each day. If you do not clean out your In Box completely, you will waste time sorting, re-reading, and handling items more often than necessary.

Use a 3-D approach for processing your In Box.

DO: Take action on important and urgent items and other items that you can process completely in two minutes or less. Do what is required and file the item.

DUMP: Immediately dump or discard any items that are not essential, important, or critical. Do not save items you do not need. Be aggressive in throwing items, including unopened obvious advertisements, into the trashcan as fast as you can.

DEFER: File all of the items that you do not resolve completely into a Pending folder. We recommend that you use a 31-day accordion folder and that you file items in the pockets for the dates you intend to process them. Alternatively, review your Pending folder once a week and process and clear out the items in it.

Use a Color-Coded Filing System

ONE OF THE SIMPLEST and fastest techniques for organizing and streamlining your work, office, and home is to use color-coding for your files.

Office supply stores offer file folders in a variety of colors to match your needs and preferences.

Colors make it easy to locate folders on your desk or in your office. Colors create a framework that makes it easy for filing items quickly.

Our Color Coding System

We use **red** folders for clients, **green** for financial and accounting, **yellow** for writing and personal, **blue** for legal, **purple** for sales and marketing, **orange** for articles and research information, and **plain manila** folders for vendors and everything else.

Tips for Using Colored Folders

- Pick colors that are meaningful to you and your projects, tasks, and areas of interest.
- Use colored folders instead of colored labels. Colored folders are affordable and they stand out better. They make filing and finding items much easier.
- Use removable labels so you can reuse folders, save money, and reduce waste.

Email Tips

EMAIL CAN be your best friend or your worst enemy. The key to effective email management is to create and follow routines, rather than being reactive. Here are a number of tips and ideas to consider:

- Turn off auto-check on your email. You cannot avoid the temptation of looking at email that automatically pings into your life. Momentary interruptions break your thoughts, divert your focus, and decrease your productivity.

- Check email only at scheduled times, such as every hour on the hour. Most people check email too often. Every 30 or 60 minutes is adequate.

- Clean out your in-box completely. If it will take more than two minutes to compose a reply, move the item to a pending file for processing later. Batch process deferred items to complete several at one sitting.

- If you do not have the time to process your in-box completely, scan for hot items that may need immediate action.

- Include a good headline, reason for the email, and required action in every email you send.

- Do not copy anyone who does not absolutely have to have the email.

How to Quit Procrastinating

PROCRASTINATION IS a big challenge and a bad habit for many people. Procrastination is avoiding doing a task or taking an action that needs to be accomplished.

Procrastination can lead to guilt, self-doubt, stress, and frustration. Procrastination can and will significantly decrease performance, results, and success.

To overcome procrastination, first acknowledge that you are a procrastinator. Then make the commitment to becoming self-disciplined and acquiring the habit of doing what must be done when it has to be done.

Our suggestion is to think less and act more. When people think too much they often find convincing excuses for why they should delay a task and do something else. When people think about a task, they talk themselves out of doing it.

Don't think about what you need to do. Just do it!

Instead of thinking about writing that report, start writing. Instead of thinking about going to the gym, get into the car and go. Instead of thinking about making your sales calls, pick up the telephone and start dialing.

A famous lawyer said that he acquired the habit of doing one thing each day that needed to be done that he did not want to do. This sounds like good advice to us.

Make Meetings Effective

A COMMON obstacle to time management that many people complain about is meetings.

Meetings are important tools; however, they have to be managed to be effective. We recommend the techniques below for eliminating unnecessary meetings and making meetings as effective as possible.

Before your meeting

- Provide a timetable and an agenda that includes a Purpose of this Meeting statement summarizing the purposes and intended outcomes.
- Send out advance reading information.

During your meeting

- Start on time and stick to the agenda.
- Use a flip chart to summarize key points so that everyone can see them.
- Do not spend time in meetings sharing basic facts or information that could have been sent out in advance of the meeting.

At the end of your meeting

- Conclude by summarizing action items, persons responsible, and due dates.
- End on time, or earlier. Do not continue a meeting longer than necessary.

It's About TIME!

The Myth of Multitasking

A PARTICIPANT came up to Jennifer after one of our *It's About TIME!* seminars. She told Jennifer she had a revelation during the program.

She explained that she has a six-year old little boy and that she had been thinking that she spends a considerable amount of time with him.

"Every day I have him play in the kitchen while I am fixing dinner, paying the bills, watching the news on the television, or talking to my mother or sisters on the telephone," she said. "That way I can multitask and save time. I can be with my son and make progress on my other chores and obligations at the same time."

"What was your revelation?" Jennifer asked.

"That I am fooling myself," she said. "When you explained your concept of chunking time in uninterrupted segments I realized that when I am multitasking I am not really spending the quality time that I was thinking I was spending with my son. I am in the same room with him physically, but not mentally. We never really connect. I'm going to change that starting tonight."

This is a good lesson for all of us. We are all so pressed to cram as much as possible into the time we have that we have been lulled into thinking that a multitasking approach is the answer.

Multitasking is not the answer. In fact, studies have shown that people who multitask actually accomplish less than those who concentrate on one task at a time.

Our observation is that when people try to multitask they dilute themselves and end up with mediocre results in everything.

The answer to time and life management is to decide what is important in life and then concentrate on those things while eliminating activities and events that are not important.

The next time you find yourself multitasking stop and ask yourself, "Where am I now, mentally?"

If you are not mentally in the same room as you are physically, maybe it is time to slow down, unplug yourself, and be where you are.

The day is always his who works in it
with serenity and great aims.

—Ralph Waldo Emerson

Don't Always Press for Perfection

QUALITY IS important; however, pressing for perfection is not always a good thing. Sometimes when you try to make something too perfect, you spend more time, effort, and resources than may be appropriate.

When you find yourself pressing for perfection, stop and think. Ask yourself if the time investment that perfection may require is worth it.

This book is an example. We would never be able to produce this or any other book that is truly perfect. We are always able to see things that we could tweak, refine, and improve. We can always read the book one more time and make one more tightening edit. However, at some point we have to say "enough" and go to print.

This does not mean that we have a that-is-good-enough philosophy. We do not.

"Good enough" as the expression is used most often never is.

However, at some point when the quality is acceptably high, the return on further investment of time may not be warranted.

Adjusting the Deck Chairs

An expression we sometimes use when we question whether we are trying to be too perfect is "are we adjusting the deck chairs?"

This is a slang referral to the ludicrous action of taking time to stop and reposition the deck chairs on a sinking ship. When a ship is sinking, perfection does not matter; what matters is getting off the ship!

If you find yourself tinkering with refinements that are not necessary instead of working on bigger and more important tasks that are critical and important, then you are adjusting the deck chairs. It is time to move on.

> *Tomorrow is the most important thing in life. Comes into us at midnight very clear. It's perfect when it arrives and it puts itself in our hands. It hopes we've learned something from yesterday.*
>
> —John Wayne

Acquire Better Habits

NOTHING THAT we have written in this book will help you manage your time better on a longer-term basis **unless you acquire the techniques as lifelong habits**.

First, Focus on Three

To acquire new time management habits we suggest that you begin with three. You can go back through this book and pick the three you like, or you can start adopting three great habits that we recommend to begin.

- **Thunderbolts:** Prepare tomorrow's daily plan using a Thunderbolt card each day before leaving work or retiring for the day.
- **Chunk your time:** Chunk at least one hour of time a day, every day, preferably in the morning, on a goal or activity that is important to you.
- **Weekly plan:** Prepare a written weekly plan every Friday for the upcoming week.

> *The beginning of a habit is like an invisible thread, but every time we repeat the act we strengthen the strand, add to it another filament, until it becomes a great cable and binds us through and through.*
>
> —Orison Swett Marden

Create a Habit Exchange Plan

After you have acquired your first three techniques as true habits, then select one to three more and acquire those as habits.

A good technique for systematically developing good habits over time is to prepare a list of the habits you intend to acquire in exchange for the habits you already have and want to discard.

Use this list as your master plan and work your plan acquiring one new habit at a time as you go down the list. This approach works for time management habits as well as for habits in other areas of your life.

We call this a habit exchange because for each new habit we desire we are exchanging a habit we have but do not want for a habit we do want.

For example, if Sherry does not currently chunk her time, she essentially is in the habit of spending her time in drabs and dribbles going from one activity to the next throughout the day. Sherry should replace her weak and ineffective old habit with a new habit of prioritizing her work and systematically working on one thing at a time, in chunks.

Improve Continually

THE FINAL strategy for working smarter is to get into the habit of continually improving.

Get into the habit of periodically stepping back and examining what you are doing and thinking and see if there might be a better way that will get the job done in a quality manner with less effort and time.

> *The only way you have a chance of working smarter is to begin by thinking smarter. The way to start thinking smarter is to ask yourself questions and then answer them.*
>
> *Look at your work and the tasks before you and ask yourself, "Is this the best way to do this? How could I get this done faster, better, or with less effort?"*
>
> —Jim Ball

Delfine's Story

DELFINE IS A sales professional of office equipment. She is in the early, formative stages of her career.

"I see myself as an organized person," Delfine said. "I have always set goals, established plans, and then pursued my goals until I achieve them."

Delfine related how she had done so well in college that she was able to play soccer, get good grades, and have a full social life as well.

"Where I can use some help is at work," Delfine explained. "I start each week with the greatest of intentions, but never seem able to accomplish everything I would like to achieve. My biggest problem is getting in all the calls I want to make. Something always comes up and I get off schedule."

Comments and analysis: In college, Delfine had set up and followed a definite structure in a disciplined manner. However, she had not carried over those good habits in her work life and no one had taken time to help her lay out a day-by-day, step-by-step approach. She was out of control and did not have a defined process to guide her.

After our discussion, Delfine went back to work, created a defined "selling system," and began to follow it rigorously. Her results improved immediately and her frustrations began to disappear.

Dos and Don'ts

Do:

- Become systematic. Take time to create processes, systems, and tools to do your work in less time. Pay particular attention to developing tools and techniques for the repeatable tasks you perform.

- Go through your office and home and throw out all the clutter that is draining your time and energy.

- Start acquiring better time management habits. Begin by focusing on three techniques in this book and acquire them as habits.

- Take steps to manage your meetings.

- Make all of your beginnings bold and strong.

Don't:

- Underestimate the drain that clutter can cause.

- Underestimate the power of creating good tools and systems to do your work.

- Try to acquire a whole bunch of new habits all at once. First, select one to three habits and take steps to acquire them. After you acquire those habits, add additional new habits you want to acquire one habit at a time until you master them.

Oh, if they would only let you work.
Wouldn't it be fine just to be able to
work? Do you know the real thing that
puts people in their little hospital cots
with nervous prostration is not working,
but trying to work and not being allowed
to. Work never hurt anybody. But this
thing of being in the middle of a letter
and then rising to shake hands with a
man who knew you when you were a
boy, and then sitting down trying to
catch the thread of that letter again—
that's what gives one general debility.

—Saunders Norvell
in *Elbert Hubbard's Scrapbook*

Authors' note: The above quote is more than 100 years old. It just goes to show you that interruptions to our work and our thoughts are age-old obstacles that successful people have always had to address and overcome.

The Three Magic
Pieces of Paper

IN STEPS 2, 3, AND 4 we described three special tools.
We refer to these as *The Three Magic Pieces of Paper*:

1. Daily time log
2. Weekly plan
3. Thunderbolts card

We have used these three tools for years. They have
helped us manage our time and achieve our goals.

Everyone gets off track once in awhile and we do,
too. However, with these three tools, we are never off
track for long and rarely do we have days when we do
not make some progress toward our primary goals.

Illustrative Blank Forms

On the following pages are illustrative forms for
each of the three tools, along with summary instructions.

If you would like to download any of these tools in
PDF file format, they are available on our website for
free at **www.goalpower.com/freetimetools.html**.

Daily Time Log Instructions

BELOW IS a recap of the instructions for preparing a Daily Time Log. Also, refer to the discussion in *Step 2: Know Where Your Time Goes*.

- Select a two or three day period to log your time.
- Start entering time in your daily time log when you arrive at work, or earlier if you prefer.
- Record a new entry in your log each time you change activities. Record the *Begin* and *End* times and a brief *Description* of your activities or tasks.
- Do not try to enter anything into your log while driving—just treat the entire trip as one activity.
- Compute the *Minutes* and enter those.
- Summarize and review your results at the end of the day. Highlight time wasters in red and effective time spent in green. Circle your chunks of time of one hour or more.
- Review your annotated log. Think through actions you can take to eliminate red items, increase your chunks of time and your green time, and improve the processes you are using.

Daily Time Log Form

Daily Time Log   Day_____ Date_____

Begin	End	Minutes	Description

Weekly Plan Instructions

BELOW IS A recap of the instructions for preparing a weekly plan. Also, refer to the discussion in *Step 3: Plan Your Weeks*.

- Set aside fifteen to twenty minutes at the end of each week to plan your next week.

- Enter the date at the top of the weekly plan and the dates for each day in the first column.

- Enter your *Goals* for the week. These should be the one to three most important goals that you intend to complete or move forward during the week.

- Think through the actions you must take to achieve your goals and enter those on the appropriate days.

- Enter any scheduled appointments or meetings that you may have or other actions that you must take during the week.

- Review your plan before the week starts and identify any actions you should take to prepare for the week. An example would be to set up a meeting.

- Follow your plan during the week.

- Evaluate your results at the end of the week. Add notes in the *Review* and *Results* section.

  Note: If you use a weekly planner-calendar, enter future appointments on the appropriate pages in your planner-calendar as you make them.

It's About TIME!

Weekly Plan Form

Week from _____ to _____

GOALS:

_____
_____
_____

SUN	
MON	
TUE	
WED	
THU	
FRI	
SAT	

Review and Results

_____
_____

Thunderbolts Card Instructions

BELOW IS a recap of instructions for preparing a Thunderbolts Card daily. Also, refer to the discussion earlier in *Step 4: Make Each Day Count*. Set aside ten minutes or so **at the end of each day** to plan tomorrow.

1. Journalize

Decide the **five (5)** most important goals or tasks you want to achieve tomorrow and enter those on your card.

2. Prioritize

Determine the order of importance of the five items and number them from 1 to 5, with 1 being the most important and 5 being the least important.

3. Visualize

Take a few moments to visualize yourself taking your Thunderbolt actions and achieving each goal or completing each task.

4. Initialize

Start work on your **number one** Thunderbolt first thing in the morning, and work on it until it is completed or as far along as you can take it. When you complete an item cross it off.

5. Finalize

Continue down your list and finalize and complete as many items during the day as you can. Review any items that you did not complete and, if appropriate, transfer them to your Thunderbolt card for the next day.

Thunderbolts Card Form

_____
(date)

_____ _____

_____ _____

_____ _____

_____ _____

_____ _____

Today's Thunderbolts

6-Week Action Plan for Success

ON THE following pages is a 6-Week Action Plan that we recommend for implementing the *5 Steps to True Time Management*.

Please note that this action plan follows an order different from the presentation of the 5 Steps in the book.

Although it is easy to learn and understand the interrelationships of the 5 Steps in the order we have presented them in this book, to apply them and adopt them as lifetime techniques, it often is best to rearrange them.

There are two reasons for this.

First, most individuals get better results and acquire new habits better when they master just a few techniques at a time rather than trying to do everything at once.

Second, to see results and maintain momentum it is best to have early successes. By learning how to use Thunderbolts, chunk your time, and say no right away, you can have early victories to keep you going.

> *Well begun is half done.*
>
> —Aristotle

> *Thunder is good, thunder is impressive, but lightning does the work.*
>
> —Mark Twain

Week 1

☐ Daily Journal and Commitment

Set up a daily journal to record your thoughts, observations, challenges, and progress. Record your commitment to managing your time better and adopting better time management habits in your journal.

☐ Thunderbolts

Start using a Thunderbolts card each day and acquiring this technique as a lifelong habit.

☐ Chunking Time

Try to schedule at least one one-hour chunk of time to devote to an important goal or activity each day. If you cannot get in one chunk a day, try to schedule at least two or three chunks in the week.

☐ Saying No

Develop a phrase you like for saying no when it is appropriate. Use the phrase to say no to unwanted and unnecessary time interruptions.

☐ Hideaway

Find and use a hideaway where you periodically can get away from everyone and everything to think and plan.

Week 2

□ **Daily Journal**
□ **Thunderbolts**
□ **Chunking Time**
□ **Saying No**
□ **Hideaway**

Continue using all of the Week 1 techniques above.
Make the commitment to acquire them as lifelong habits.
Be persistent and stick with them. If you get off track
and do not use one or more techniques in any given day,
start right up the next day and get on track.

□ Weekly Plan

Start using the weekly planning technique as a lifelong
habit by preparing a weekly plan for next week.

□ Clutter

Set aside a few hours, a half-day, a few days, or whatever time you need to clean out the physical clutter you
may have in your life at home and at work. Schedule this
time in your weekly plan. Then on the appointed days,
clean out your clutter!

If you have a lot of clutter, try scheduling a few
hours each week to clean out your clutter and continue
this until you are clutter free!

Week 3

☐ Daily Journal
☐ Thunderbolts
☐ Chunking Time
☐ Saying No
☐ Hideaway
☐ Weekly Plan

Continue using all these techniques. Make the commitment to acquire them as lifelong habits. Be persistent and stick with them. If you get off track and do not use one or more techniques in any given day, start right up the next day and get on track.

Start expanding the time that you spend in chunks with people and on important goals and activities.

☐ Time Wants, Priorities, and Goals

Think through your time wants and prioritize them. Then select and quantify the specific time goals and plans that you want to achieve. Write these in your daily journal.

Week 4

☐ **Daily Journal**
☐ **Thunderbolts**
☐ **Chunking Time**
☐ **Saying No**
☐ **Hideaway**
☐ **Weekly Plan**

Continue using all these techniques so they become life-long habits. Be persistent and stick with them. If you get off track and do not use one or more techniques in any given day, start right up the next day and get on track.

☐ Time Log

Select two or three typical days and prepare a daily time log for those days. Next, summarize and analyze your results. Then decide what actions you must take to change things so that you manage your time better.

Week 5

- ☐ Daily Journal
- ☐ Thunderbolts
- ☐ Chunking Time
- ☐ Saying No
- ☐ Hideaway
- ☐ Weekly Plan

Continue using all these techniques so they become life-long habits. Be persistent and stick with them. If you get off track and do not use one or more techniques in any given day, start right up the next day and get on track.

☐ Create Better Processes and Tools

Think through the tasks and work that you do and identify the repeatable processes you follow where you could improve the process or create tools to help you do more in less time. Take time to create and use the tools.

☐ Acquire Better Habits

Create a habit exchange plan by listing the habits you want to acquire in exchange for those you want to discard. Then systematically work your plan by acquiring one new habit at a time until you have acquired all the habits you desire.

Week 6

☐ **Daily Journal**
☐ **Thunderbolts**
☐ **Chunking Time**
☐ **Saying No**
☐ **Hideaway**
☐ **Weekly Plan**

Continue using all these techniques so they become life-long habits. Be persistent and stick with them. If you get off track and do not use one or more techniques in any given day, start right up the next day and get on track.

☐ Review

Go back through this book and your notes to review the concepts. Refine your approach in using the techniques.

☐ Congratulations!

Congratulations! You have just implemented the *5 Steps to True Time Management* and you are on an excellent path to success and happiness!

Carpe Diem!

CONGRATULATIONS! You have just finished reading *It's About TIME! 5 Steps to True Time Management.* You now are on a new journey with excellent tools and knowledge to guide your way.

We know that the principles and concepts in this book will help you manage your time better so that you can spend more of it the way you want to spend it, get more done each day, and have more fun along the way.

Carpe Diem!

We began this book with a little story about Julius Caesar's servant reminding him, "Thou art mortal."

This was a reminder for Caesar that time is life.

Another reminder, in Latin and perhaps from Caesar himself, is *Carpe Diem!*

Seize the day!

The five steps and related principles and concepts in this book cannot help you if you do not apply them and adopt them as routines and habits for your life.

Seize the day and start immediately!

Do not put off for a single day beginning to apply the five steps in this book.

Begin now!

Free Resources

The Three Magic Pieces of Paper — Free Forms

To help get you started on your road to better time management, you may obtain printable versions of blank forms for each of the *The Three Magic Pieces of Paper* described in this book. To obtain the forms free of charge visit **www.goalpower.com/freetimetools.html**.

Free Ballgrams®

Ballgrams are periodic stories, tips, and ideas for success in business and life from Jim Ball. Jim writes these every week or so and we email them free of charge. To subscribe, visit **www.goalpower.com**.

Free Articles and Tips

The Goals Institute provides free articles on goal achievement, motivation, personal performance, and other topics on its website. Visit **www.goalpower.com**.

It is not enough to be busy; so are the ants.
The question is: What are we busy about?

—Henry David Thoreau

About the Authors

JAMES R. BALL is CEO and JENNIFER A. KUCHTA (cook-ta) is Vice President of The Goals Institute, the company they founded to help businesses and organizations achieve their potential through goal achievement.

Jim and Jennifer write books, develop learning programs, and provide speeches and seminars for organizations.

James R. Ball

Previously, Jim was co-founder and CEO of Venture America, a venture capital firm that helped launch more than twenty companies, including The Discovery Channel.

Before that, he was a managing partner at Arthur Andersen. He has been an adjunct faculty member at George Mason University where he co-founded George Mason University Entrepreneurial Institute, Inc.

Jim is a certified public accountant and member of the American Institute of Certified Public Accountants. He and his wife Dolly live in Virginia. They have two adult daughters, Jennifer and Stephanie.

Jennifer A. Kuchta

Previously, Jennifer oversaw finance, administration, investor relations, and services and support of portfolio companies at Venture America.

Before that, she was a marketing support specialist for sales representatives of fine arts. She has an accounting degree and is a member of several business organizations.

Other Books by the Authors[*]

Keep It Simple for Success® is a series of books and learning programs authored and developed by Jim Ball and Jennifer Kuchta and published by The Goals Institute. The titles in the series as of the date of publication of this book are*:

ABCs for Life

Goal Power®

It's About TIME!

Professionalism Is for Everyone

World-Class Customer Service

Additional books by Jim Ball:

Soar . . . If You Dare®

DNA Leadership through Goal-Driven Management

The Entrepreneur's Tool Kit

*Additional books are forthcoming. For a current listing of all titles, please visit our website at **www.goalpower.com**.

Index

Seminars and
Train-the-Trainer Programs

WE PROVIDE SEMINARS AND TRAIN-THE-TRAINER facilitator and participant materials on various topics including the content of our books *It's About TIME!*, *Professionalism Is for Everyone*, *Goal Power*®, *World-Class Customer Service*, *DNA Leadership through Goal-Driven Management*, and *Soar . . . If You Dare*®.

If you would like more information about our programs, our other book titles, discounts for volume purchases, our speaking services, our train-the-trainer approach and offerings, or if you would like to send us your comments or suggestions, please contact us:

The Goals Institute
703-264-2000

www.goalpower.com
www.goalsinstitute.com
www.kissbooks.com

email: info@goalsinstitute.com